Things TO DO in YOUNG PEOPLE'S WORSHIP

BOOK 3

SUSAN SAYERS

Kevin Mayhew

First published in 2000 by
KEVIN MAYHEW LTD
Buxhall
Stowmarket
Suffolk IP14 3BW

Things To Do in Young People's Worship, Book 3, is adapted from *Living Stones, Boulders, Years A, B and C,* by Susan Sayers, published by Kevin Mayhew, 1999.

0 1 2 3 4 5 6 7 8 9

ISBN 1 84003 537 4
Catalogue No 1500349

Cover design by Jonathan Stroulger
Edited by Peter Dainty
Typesetting by Louise Selfe
Printed in Great Britain

Foreword

While many churches provide for the needs of children, there is often an uncomfortable gap where young people are concerned. This is the age when deep questions are being asked, and it is essential that our young people find in their churches those who are going to listen and not be shocked; who are willing to enter into real discussion and provide relevant and unsuffocating support during adolescence.

Many churches are well aware of the needs, but find it difficult to provide for them. They are concerned about this age group feeling too old for children's ministry but not able to relate to what the adults are doing in church. Sadly, the result is often an exodus of young people, just when their faith could be (and often is) taking off.

Not only do our young people need the Church; the Church badly needs its young people. Their insistence on rejecting every hint of hypocrisy and their gift of presenting challenging ideas with wit and enthusiasm – these are good for everyone and vital for a healthy body of Christ.

This book aims to provide relevant and varied activities for young people, which stimulate their thinking and encourage valuable discussion. Although some young people will be involved in the children's ministry team, I am convinced that they need to be provided for at their own level as well. Sometimes I have suggested that the young people put their ideas to the wider Church. Do encourage the Church to take such ideas seriously.

A note about role-play

Improvising a drama is a very effective way of helping people get 'under the skin' of Bible and other stories. Precisely because of that, it is vitally important for the leader to 'de-role' the actors after it. This is simply and effectively done if the leader goes round the group asking each one to say his or her name, where they are and to define their real relationship with other actors, e.g:

What's your name?
Joanna Harrison.

Where are you?
Bethany Baptist Church youth group.

And do you *really* hate Karen?

No, that was just an act. We're friends.

This can be done in a very light-hearted way, adding to the fun of the role-play itself, and may seem quite trivial. However, for people of any age who have 'thought themselves into' a part, it's absolutely essential they 'talk themselves out of it'.

I hope the ideas in this book will enable young people in the churches to grow strong and healthy in their faith.

Recommended Bibles

It is often a good idea to look at a passage in several different versions before deciding which to use for a particular occasion, especially if you plan to involve several people in the reading.

For young people the New Century version of *The Youth Bible* includes various anecdotes and Bible studies which are inviting and challenging. A vivid version of the New Testament and parts of the Old Testament in contemporary language is Eugene Peterson's *The Message*. This catches the imagination and aids understanding. It is particularly good for reading aloud. *Into the Light* by the Bible Society is specially developed for reading aloud to those unused to the traditional language of the Church.

SUSAN SAYERS

Contents

The Living God

God Incarnate

Thought for the day

Just as the angels said, a Saviour has been born for us.

Things to read

Galatians 4:4-7
Luke 2:15-21

Things to do

The Trinity is discussing the Incarnation. Father, Son and Spirit are seated as in the icon of the Holy Trinity. (Sounds of arguments and war.)

The Father What they need is the Spirit of God actually alive in them.

The Spirit That's a very personal thing. How can it be done?

The Son Well, as it's personal, it'll have to be done in person.

The Father That's true.

The Spirit It will mean them meeting the Spirit of God in a human person.

(The Father and the Spirit both look at the Son.)

All three speak together:
That's where you/I come in.

The Son How long for?

The Father It'll happen in stages. First, a year or two in ministry, tied to one time zone and in one area, till they get the hang of it.

The Spirit They won't be able to cope for long with God among them in person.

The Father Exactly. It's bound to end in them expelling you.

The Son You mean killing me?

The Father Sadly, yes. But that opens up a new possibility – stage two.

The Spirit How do you mean?

The Father Our love is stronger than death and cannot be destroyed. Through your risen life the Spirit of God will be available for every person in every place and every time zone.

The Spirit So no one needs to lose out!

The Son They'll be able to live the heaven life while they're alive on earth as well as after death!

The Father That's right!

The Son If I'm going to do a couple of years of Godly ministry as a human, I'll have to do all the growing-up bit as well, won't I?

The Father Oh yes – right from conception; you'll need to be part of the whole human experience.

The Spirit But babies are very vulnerable. Suppose they kill him too early?

The Father It's a risk. It's all a risk.

All But if we don't take it, they'll be thrashing about in the dark for ever. They can't save themselves. They need a Saviour.

Human voices, praying earnestly for help:

O come, O come, Emmanuel, save us and set us free!

The Son It's those faithful watchmen calling again.

All And the time is right. Everything's ready.

The Father Gabriel! Come here a moment, will you. We've got some important messages which need delivering personally . . .

Follow this by reading the passage from Galatians 4, which links up with the sketch.

Now explain how shepherds were considered 'unclean' outsiders because their job meant they were often in contact with dead bodies, and their working hours made it impossible for them to take a full part in the community's worship. Bearing this in mind, read the Gospel for today.

Things to discuss

1. Really good news alters lives. Share with the group any such news you remember receiving. Bearing in mind the religious standing of the shepherds, how might they feel on hearing the angels' news, and then on discovering the baby in the manger?

2. What factors can we see, with hindsight, which made this time 'right' for Jesus to be born?

God's Mysterious Nature

Thought for the day

The mysterious and holy nature of the one true God is beyond our understanding, but it is both communal harmony and individual personality, Father, Son and Holy Spirit.

Things to read

Isaiah 6:1-4
John 3:1-17

Things to do

Who are you? The group is going to discover as much as possible about you in five minutes. Before the timing starts, let them collectively establish what they do know about you already, so the question time isn't wasted. Explain that if you don't want to answer a particular question you will say so; but they can ask whatever they want to in order to get to know who you are and what you are like.

Look back at how the group discovered more about you. They ran their minds over what they knew already and went on from there. Were there some things they thought they knew which turned out to be mistaken? Were they surprised by any of the new discoveries?

Today we are focusing on who God is and what he is like. Collectively as a Church, over the years, some clear truths about God have been discovered:

- God is One Being
- God is Three Persons – Father, Son and Holy Spirit.

(Trinity means Tri-Unity, or Three in One and One in Three.)

Why does the Church describe God in this way? Look together at what they know of God as Father, Son and Spirit, to see how the concept of Trinity has developed, referring to these passages to help: Genesis 1:1-3; Isaiah 9:6; Luke 1:35; John 10:36-38; John 14:25-26.

Finally read John 3:1-17 to see how the invisible nature of the wind helps Nicodemus discover more about the nature of God.

Things to discuss

1. How does each Person of the Trinity testify to the others?
2. What would you like God to enable you to 'see'?

The Word Made Flesh

Thought for the day

The Word made flesh at Christmas was always with God, always expressing his creative love.

Things to read

Psalm 33:4-7
Proverbs 8:22-31
John 1:(1-9) 10-18

Things to do

Play hangman, where the word is there already and just needs them to uncover it.

First read the Gospel for today, noticing the capital W in Word and discussing who John is talking about. In what way is Jesus God's Word? Was God's Word there at the beginning, as John says? (Look at Genesis 1 to check.)

Now look at the Old Testament readings, picking up on the Word (sometimes thought of as the wisdom of God) being there all the time and not suddenly arriving on the hay in Bethlehem from nowhere.

Explain how John was writing for the Greek philosophers who would find it helpful to think of God in this way. Link it, too, with what God called himself when talking to Moses (Exodus 3:13-15) and with Jesus' 'I AM' teaching (John 8:58, for example).

Encourage them to explore the beginning of John's Gospel more deeply, expressing their ideas in drawing.

Things to discuss

1. Why do you think the eternal Word came into our world as a human baby, born as vulnerable and dependent as the rest of us?
2. How does our faith in Jesus affect the way we look at the books of the Old Testament?

God's Glory Revealed

Thought for the day

Jesus is glorified both on the mountain and on the cross.

Things to read

Isaiah 40:3-5
Mark 9:2-9

Things to do

Beforehand prepare a message which they can communally discover by making a rubbing of it. (Cut out each letter of the message from cardboard and stick the letters on a card or paper base. Cover the whole thing with lining paper, secured with sticky tape.) Give everyone wax crayons to rub over the lining paper in order to see the message:

NOW YOU HAVE SEEN
THE HIDDEN MESSAGE!

Point out that the message was just as much there before they saw it; it was simply hidden from view. Today we are going to look at a time when God's glory became very obvious in Jesus. Read Mark's account of the Transfiguration on the mountain top. Think over what it revealed about Jesus, what it made clear and plain. (That Jesus was God's Son; he was filled with God's glory; he had God's authority; he was fulfilling the Law and the prophets; suffering and death had to be part of the rescue plan.)

How else in his life did Jesus show God's glory, but not by literally 'shining' with it? (In the way he spoke and taught; the way he healed and comforted; and, above all, in being willing to die a cursed death on the cross.)

Look at what John says about this in his Gospel (John 1:14) and what the prophet Isaiah said in Isaiah 40:3-5.

Also read Exodus 3:2, Exodus 13:21 and Exodus 19:18. Notice how the image of shining brightness and fire is seen as a sign of God's presence.

Things to discuss

1. Are we wary of God showing his glory, preferring to 'tone him down'?
2. How do you think the Transfiguration helped the disciples who witnessed it?

Signs of Glory

Thought for the day

Signs of glory lead us to believe in Jesus as Lord and Saviour.

Things to read

Genesis 14:17-20
Psalm 128
Revelation 19:6-10
John 2:1-11

Things to do

Play 'Give us a clue', where signs are used to describe a film, book or TV programme title. Also have the following signs on display around the room:

Read the story of the wedding at Cana, with different people reading the various parts. Explore the meaning of the story, establishing who was there, what each did, where it happened, and what it shows us about Jesus.

This leads on to the reading from Revelation, where the everlasting authority and worth of Jesus are affirmed. Read it together, looking out for the way it confirms what we have glimpsed in this first miracle of Jesus.

Things to discuss

1. If you had no church background, which events of the Gospels would lead you to consider worshipping Jesus as Lord?
2. Look at the different characters in the Cana wedding event and discuss what might have been going through their minds at each stage of the episode.

God's Justice and Mercy

Thought for the day

God's justice is always blended with mercy and loving kindness, so that we have real hope.

Things to read

1 Kings 3:5-28
Psalm 103:6-13
Romans 8:18-25
Matthew 13:24-30, 36-43

Things to do

Aim: To know that God's nature is to be both just and merciful. Give out a number of crimes, and decide on appropriate punishments for them. Here are some crime ideas:

- Taking the rest of a chocolate biscuit pack that had only had two biscuits previously eaten.
- Borrowing a favourite sweater and getting a mark on it.
- Copying your essay and getting a higher mark for it than it originally got.
- Playing football in the street and accidentally breaking a neighbour's stained-glass window.
- Playing a dud tape in a friend's video so that it dirties the heads and won't play clearly.

If you are found guilty in a court, a punishment has to be decided on which is fair and just. Today we are looking at where our desire to be fair comes from.

First read the passage from Psalm 103. What has the writer discovered about God's nature? That he is both just and kind-hearted; that from his position of power and strength he chooses to act with leniency and mercy. If you have time read 1 Kings 3:5-28 as well, which shows how Solomon put into practice the wise justice he had received from God.

Since God is obviously just, how come there is so much evil and suffering in the world, much of which seems to go unchecked?

Read Romans 8:18-25, with its picture of the whole universe groaning in childbirth, and the great conviction of hope even in the middle of suffering. Then look at the parable Jesus told about the wheat and weeds, where, out of loving concern, the evil is allowed to continue at the moment, but it will not be so for ever.

Ultimately, all that is good will be saved, and all that is evil will be destroyed. And in one sense, all of us belong to the kingdom now as well as then. God's people are called to right injustice and 'champion the unwanted' here and now.

Things to discuss

1. How would you answer someone who took all the terrible natural disasters as evidence that God is not merciful but cruel?

2. Can mercy sometimes prevent us from growing up and facing our responsibilities?

God's Kindness and Gentleness

Thought for the day

To all who are weary with carrying heavy burdens in life, Jesus offers rest for our souls and unthreatening relief.

Things to read

Zechariah 9:9-10
Psalm 145:8-14
Matthew 11:16-19, 25-30

Things to do

Aim: To look at how we need to be childlike to accept God's love, but not childish.

Animal, plant, sweet. In a circle someone starts by saying, 'If this person were an animal they would be a . . . ; if they were a plant they would be a . . . ; and if they were a sweet they would be a . . .' Then everyone has to guess who it is. You can either stick to the people in the group for this, or have particular categories such as singers, sports personalities or film stars.

We were able to work out some of those (or not, as the case may be!) because the animals, plants and fruit were chosen to sum up what the particular person is like. In the time that the book of Zechariah was written, certain animals had certain images that the people would relate to. A horse, for instance, was a symbol of war and power, and a donkey was a symbol of peace and humility. Read the passage from Zechariah, noticing how the image of a donkey is used, and what idea is being put across by this about the promised Messianic king. Remind them of how Jesus chose to enter Jerusalem many years later, so they can see the connection.

Look at the qualities of God which are listed in Psalm 145, and notice how these link up with the expected Messiah and Jesus riding into Jerusalem. At this point also read Matthew 11:28-30, as this, too, expresses those same qualities in action. (It is a passage that they could learn by heart to have with them at all times.)

But do people take Jesus up on this offer? Some do, some don't. Go back to Matthew 11:16-19 to hear Jesus getting a bit exasperated by the childish behaviour of some of the religious leaders. Then read verses 25-26. The ones who are not too self-satisfied or proud of their cleverness, but are able to look at things in a direct, open, childlike way, are the ones who understand what Jesus is talking about, and can enjoy receiving the gifts God wants to give.

Things to discuss

1. When Jesus chose to enter Jerusalem on a donkey, what was he consciously trying to show the people of Israel?
2. What is the difference between childish and childlike behaviour, and why does being childlike make it possible for us to respond to God's wisdom?

The Image of God

Thought for the day

Christ is the image of the unseen God, the first-born of all creation.

Things to read

Proverbs 8:1, 22-31
Colossians 1:15-20
John 1:1-14

Things to do

Have an assortment of minerals, plants and shells for them to identify, using suitable reference books.

Read the first four verses from John 1, with the objects they have been identifying spread out on calendar pictures of the world's beauty, while you read. Look at how complex and organised, varied and extraordinary that creation is. The objects and pictures are just a very few examples of it all.

John is saying that the person we know as Jesus Christ, although he became flesh at that point in time, had always been there, right from the beginning – in fact, just as his earthly life expresses God, so at the creation it was this 'expressive Word' with which God spoke the universe into being.

Now look at the reading from Colossians. Paul is quoting an early hymn, which is thinking over the same idea that we've just read in the introduction to John's Gospel. Check the similarities together.

In Proverbs, in the Old Testament, 'wisdom' is described in similar terms: she is with God at the beginning and shared in his work of creation. So Christians sometimes call Jesus the wisdom of God, as well as the Word and image of God.

We can go around most of the time with our heads down, occupied with all the everyday things like eating, socialising and spending money, but sometimes it suddenly occurs to us to ask ourselves what we're here for, and how we come to be whizzing round on this particular chunk of solidified gases in the universe. If we start looking and listening to what is all around us, we notice the distinctive mark of the God who created it; the mark of a wise and all-powerful Being, full of love.

Things to discuss

God created people in his own image as both male and female; Wisdom and the Spirit are both referred to as 'she', and the Word of God became flesh as a male. What do we miss if our understanding of God is predominantly 'male'?

The Spirit at Work

Thought for the day

The Holy Spirit changed the disciples and still changes Jesus' followers now.

Things to read

Acts 2:1-21

Things to do

All change! Have a selection of scarves and hats, enough for everyone and as silly as you like. Use a CD-player for music so that you can skip from track to track. When the music starts, each person dresses up. Whenever the track changes, they have to swap their hat and scarf with someone else.

Explain that the disciples had seen a lot of changes in the last few years of their lives. Jesus had called them out of their normal jobs, they'd travelled around to different places, changed their way of thinking and their way of thinking about God. They'd lived through the crucifixion, Jesus being dead and Jesus being alive again. Now they were waiting for another change, not quite knowing what the Holy Spirit would do to them, but knowing it was important to be ready for it.

Now read from Acts.

What has happened to the disciples with the coming of the Holy Spirit? How are they behaving? How are they different? Why are they so excited? What was it they wanted everyone to know?

And the Holy Spirit is still changing people today. Act out the following sketch.

ACTS TOO

Beth: Have you noticed how Dave's changed over the last few months?

Ryan: Yes, I have. He seems more settled. And he doesn't keep losing his temper.

Carl: He lost it last week though.

Ryan: Yeah, but that was when he got mad at Ross for kicking my shirt into the gutter.

Beth: In the old days it would have been Dave doing the shirt kicking!

Carl: What's happened, do you reckon?

Ryan: Well, we've all been praying for him, haven't we? And he's been asking questions about things as well.

Beth: What things?

Ryan: Oh, you know – who made God... what are ghosts... that kind of stuff.

Carl: God's amazing. Fancy him listening to our prayers.

Beth: Yes, and he's sorting Dave out. God's power is so incredible.

All: God does things. God ACTS TOO.

Carl: Acts 2! That's today's reading!

Things to discuss

1. Why isn't the Holy Spirit poured out more than it is in our own church? What can we learn from the disciples' expectant waiting?
2. Do we try to impose restrictions or guidelines for the Holy Spirit in case our lives are too much challenged by too much of God's presence?

The Holy Spirit

Thought for the day

Through the Holy Spirit, Jesus is affirmed at his Baptism as God's beloved Son, and we too are given the Spirit of God which affirms us as God's adopted daughters and sons.

Things to read

Genesis 1:1-5
Acts 19:1-7
Mark 1:4-11

Things to do

Play the beginning of Haydn's Creation and give out paper and paints for them to express it in colour and form. As they paint, read the Genesis account above the music.

Where is the Spirit of God in this passage? (Look at verse 2.) Point out that God cannot exist apart from his Spirit – the Holy Spirit is like the life, or breath, of God.

Now read Mark's account of Jesus' Baptism, noticing how the Spirit of God is portrayed here, and exploring why it might have seemed like a dove. Link this with the words God speaks to affirm Jesus in his identity and his mission.

Read Acts 19:1-7; in what ways is the Holy Spirit coming as at creation and at Jesus' Baptism? What are its effects? When *we* sense God's presence, is it like this or different again? Help them to see that God's Spirit comes to fill us only when we genuinely seek God and long to be filled with his life. How the Spirit comes varies, but always there is a sense of inner peace and joy, a deepening of love for God and a deepening realisation that God is real, alive and active.

Things to discuss

1. Why do you think Jesus was baptised by John when he didn't need to repent?
2. Is the thought of God's Spirit dwelling in us a little frightening; would we prefer God to keep his distance?

Jesus Our Lord

Jesus the Messiah

Thought for the day

In Jesus, God fulfilled the Messianic prophecies about the promised Saviour.

Things to read

Isaiah 61:1-4, 8-11
Acts 2:22-24, 36
John 1:6-8, 19-22

Things to do

Each person in turn adds a word to a gradually developing sentence, so that some kind of story starts to take shape, which no one person has planned.

All through the history of the people of Israel words were spoken by the prophets to reveal a bit more about what God meant and what God was like. Gradually the people started to grasp that one day God would be among his people to save them, in a new and very personal way. They started to think in terms of a Messiah, one anointed by God, who would come to them.

Look at the reading from Isaiah 61 to discover what the Messiah would be like. Pick out the characteristics in discussion and make a note of them. Then look at today's Gospel. Why might they have thought that John was the Messiah or Elijah? (You can refer to the notes made.) Then read on to find out how John describes himself. Link this with the passage from Isaiah which you've just read. Why did John talk about the Messiah being already among them, though not yet known? (Think back to when John and Jesus had been born.)

Then read the passage from Peter's sermon in Acts. The task of the apostles was to make clear to all who would listen that Jesus was the Messiah.

Things to discuss

1. Why did the authorities want to check out John's identity and authority?
2. What was it that made the first disciples realise that Jesus was the promised Messiah?

Raising the Dead

Thought for the day

God's power can reach even into death and draw out life.

Things to read

2 Samuel 1:1, 17-27
Mark 5:21-43

Things to do

Use a stopwatch and set someone off talking for one minute on a particular subject. They can be interrupted and challenged for repetitions or hesitations, after which the challenger continues the talk. Whoever is talking at time-up is the winner.

Putting the reading in context, look first at 2 Samuel 1, and talk a little together about how sad it is when someone we know and love dies, and how we miss seeing them.

Now make a point of moving from the Old to the New Testament, and read Mark 5:21-43. Read it with different voices taking the various parts. Are they surprised at Jesus actually raising the dead? What does this show his followers? Why do they think only a few were allowed to be present?

Also look at the healing which takes place on the way to Jairus' house. How do they think Jairus might have been feeling while Jesus took time to talk to the woman? How do they cope with urgent interruptions? What if the interruption was the reason the little girl was already dead – might this be why Jesus was prepared to bring her back from the dead?

Finally look at what Mark shows us about faith. Where does faith and believing come up in the two healings of today's Gospel? What does Jesus say about it?

Things to discuss

The situation in the Gospel of urgent business being interrupted by another crisis is all too familiar! What can we learn from Jesus' way of dealing with it?

Understanding Jesus

Thought for the day

As Jesus is baptised, the Spirit of God rests visibly on him, marking him out as the One who will save his people.

Things to read

Isaiah 42:1-9
Acts 10:34-43
Matthew 3:13-17

Things to do

Aim: To see Jesus gradually being revealed as the fulfilment of God's promises.

Jigsaw puzzles. These can be done on their own or in pairs, or in a larger group, without the picture to help, so that the understanding of the picture gradually becomes apparent.

Start by reading the prophecy from Isaiah, asking them to think of who it reminds them of. (Whoever the prophet was referring to at the time, Jesus certainly saw it as fitting in exactly with his own role.)

Take particular note of the opening verses, and then read Matthew's account of Jesus' Baptism, listening out for any echoes of the Isaiah passage. They are now getting an idea of what it was like for the Jewish people to hear and read Matthew's Gospel – they would pick up on familiar passages from Scripture which would help them to understand the way Jesus fulfilled the old prophecies. They could begin to see God's plan taking shape through history, and everything coming together in Jesus of Nazareth. You may like to look at the Gospel translation in *The Message,* as this expresses, as part of the text, what you have been discovering.

Now try this short sketch. Set up an optician (white-coated) with examination chair facing the audience. Optician has a torch, and mimes giving the eye examination. The audience see the words up behind the client.

Optician Ah, good afternoon, madam. If you'd like to sit down here . . .

Client Oh, thanks. I hope this won't take too long. I'm late already.

Optician Just read me the letters on the board, madam.

Client J, E, S, U, S / I, S / T, H, E / O, N, E / W, E / A, R, E / W, A, I, T, I, N, G / F, O, R.

Optician Excellent sight, madam! Every letter clear to the very small print at the bottom.

Client Can I go now, then?

Optician What about the message, though? Can you read the message?

Client Message – what message?

Optician The one staring you in the eye, madam. You can see it clearly enough.

Client No, I can't see any message. Does that mean I need glasses?

Optician *(writing on her record card)* Physical sight: perfect. Spiritual sight: nil.

Things to discuss

1. What links are there between the Isaiah passage and the subsequent ministry of Jesus?
2. How does Peter explain what happened at Jesus' Baptism (Acts 10:38)? What is the significance of 'anointing'?

Calming the Storm

Thought for the day

What kind of person is this? Even the wind and waves obey him.

Things to read

Psalm 107:23-32
Mark 4:35-41

Things to do

What are we? Explain that they are some kind of group with some kind of leader, and they can work out what they are by asking the leader questions (yes/no answers only). They may be objects, animals or people, or a combination. To start them off they are given one clue.

Here are some possible scenarios:

- Swallows perched on a telegraph wire gathering in the autumn for their leader to set them off on migration to Africa. (Clue: a feather)
- Members of a morris dance team with the leader playing an accordion. (Clue: bells and a white hanky)
- A mountain rescue team in thick fog on Snowdon guided by the compass. (Clue: A map and a first aid kit)

What does it mean for God to be in charge? First read Psalm 107:23-32, looking at it from this point of view. Notice that God is in the power of the storm as well as in the calming of the storm.

Now read from Mark's Gospel the account of Jesus calming the wind and waves.

Why do they think the disciples woke Jesus up?

Do they think they would all have drowned if Jesus hadn't commanded the weather to calm down?

Why might Jesus have chosen to do this instead of comforting the disciples and cheering them through the difficult situation? (Feeling compassion for them?/ showing a sign?/fighting with evil?)

What did it help the disciples to understand about Jesus in a very dramatic lesson?

What does it help us to see about Jesus as we read the account two thousand years later?

Share ideas and other questions they may have.

Invite them to look at possible storms into which Jesus speaks calm – in their own lives, in the Church and in the news.

Things to discuss

1. When were you last stunned by the awesome power of the living God? Share your experiences and how they affected your understanding of God.
2. If people know something of what God is really like, how is it likely to affect the way they pray?

The Bread of Life

Thought for the day

Jesus is the Bread of Life who satisfies our hunger and sustains us on our journey to heaven.

Things to read

Exodus 16:2-3, 11-21
John 6:24-35

Things to do

This person . . . Sit in a circle, and take it in turns to describe someone (who may be famous, or someone everyone knows), not by looks but by different things they do or have done. Whoever guesses the identity can have the next go.

We managed to work out who those people were without knowing anything about their appearance. We know hardly anything about Jesus' appearance, but we can tell a great deal about him by what he said and did. Today we're going to look at one of the ways Jesus described himself.

Read today's Gospel, writing 'I am the Bread of Life' on a large sheet as it comes up. Talk about what Jesus might have meant by this. (Look at what bread does for our physical bodies and then look at how Jesus does this in a spiritual way – feeding, satisfying hunger, providing essentials for growth and health and energy, and so on.)

Now look back to the Exodus passage referred to in the Gospel, so that they can see the connection and the background to the way Jesus was thinking. Who did the people think had provided them with manna in the desert? (Look at Jesus' reply in John 6:32.) Remembering how the crowd had just recently been miraculously fed by Jesus, talk about what they might have meant in verse 30 of John 6. What does it mean to 'believe in the one God sent'? (Verse 29)

Point out that we all walk straight past things we're not prepared or expecting to see, and some of the people couldn't believe that Jesus could be anywhere near as holy as Moses, the holy figure from the past. They didn't realise that Moses had been pointing towards this moment, and that they happened to be alive at the very time God's Son came to the earth.

Things to discuss

1. Do we realise our need of Jesus' feeding, or think of it more as an optional extra?
2. How can our God-given work in life just be to believe in Jesus? (What difference does that belief make to everything else we do?)

Jesus Feeds Us

Thought for the day

Out of God's riches, a great crowd is fed and satisfied from a small offering of food.

Things to read

2 Kings 4:42-44
1 Corinthians 11:23-26
John 6:1-13

Things to do

Bread tasting. Bring a selection of breads from different parts of the world, together with an atlas or world map. Find where each bread comes from and sample it. All over the world bread of some kind is basic food.

Begin by reading the passage from 2 Kings, where Elisha feeds a hundred people with a gift of bread. Notice the generosity (in offering the bread) and Elisha's careful listening to God's will, and his wholehearted obedience to it.

Now look at the feeding of the five thousand in John's Gospel. Draw attention to the timing – it's about Passover time. (Another meal, just before the escape from slavery.) Look at what Jesus does with the food – he accepts the gift, gives thanks to God for it, breaks it in pieces and gives it out to the people to feed them when they are hungry.

Link this with what Jesus started at the Passover meal he shared with his disciples before his death (see 1 Corinthians 11:23-26), and which goes on happening in all our churches right through the centuries and the generations, all over the world. That is quite a crowd being fed! And we are part of that same blessing, breaking and giving out which has been going on for two thousand years. It's a record-breaking meal.

Things to discuss

1. When faced with our next problem which looks insurmountable, how can today's Gospel help us do things God's way?
2. What do you think is the meaning of the twelve baskets of leftovers?

The Good Shepherd

Thought for the day

'I am the Good Shepherd and I lay down my life for the sheep.'

Things to read

Ezekiel 34:1-15
Psalm 23
John 10:11-18

Things to do

Role-call. Give out identities to particular people, which they keep secret. Then provide a situation which they all act out in role. Onlookers have to guess the identities/ characters from the way they are acting. (Example – travelling on a train: someone with chicken pox, a spy, a *Sun* reporter looking for a story, and the Queen travelling incognito.)

Jesus knew the scriptures and what had been written about the Messiah in the books of the prophets, and the Psalms. There was quite a lot about God's shepherding (read Psalm 23) and the Messiah would be a kind of Shepherd King, like David. (Have a look at a few examples, such as Psalm 28:9; Ezekiel 34:15; Isaiah 40:11.) There was also a recurring theme of the false shepherding of God's people, who were left as sheep without a shepherd (Ezekiel 34:5). In Mark and Matthew, Jesus is said to have compassion on the people because of this (Matthew 9:36 and Mark 6:34).

So now, with this background, look at today's Gospel, John 10:11-18. Jesus is not only showing his disciples the example of the real shepherds around on the hills where they were living. He is also directing them to see how he is fulfilling the prophets and the Psalms as the real, authentic leader of God's people, in contrast to those who are only out for themselves, and are not listening carefully to God.

Things to discuss

1. Does our lack of trust in the Good Shepherd and our lack of expectation prevent his work being done?
2. How has God led and protected us in our lives (as individuals and as a church)?

For and Against

Thought for the day

Jesus had both enemies and friends.

Things to read

Joshua 24:14-24
Mark 3:20-35

Things to do

Play 'netball' using a blow-up beach ball and a bucket or bin for the net. Play first with even sides, and then with everyone on the same side, and no opponents. Compare the scores!

It is so much easier to score goals when we don't have any opposition! Today we are going to look at some opposition Jesus was faced with, and how he dealt with it.

It wasn't just when Jesus was around that people had to decide whether they were on God's side or not. Read the passage from Joshua to see an example of that.

Now read today's Gospel, looking out for any friction and opposition to his work. There are two main areas in this reading – the accusation of the scribes, and the concerned family, coming to 'take charge' of Jesus.

What do the scribes accuse Jesus of doing? (Casting out demons by the power of demons.) Would this make logical sense? How does Jesus respond to what they are saying about him? (If Satan was fighting against himself in that way, his power would crash.) Logic proves that Jesus cannot be in league with Satan if he is overcoming evil spirits in people.

What about his family – why have they come, and why doesn't Jesus rush off home with them as they would like? Having heard the reports of the crowds surrounding Jesus all the time, giving him no time even to eat, and all the casting-out of evil spirits, they are anxious for him and don't understand that his work on earth is very important, and needs to be done, even if it's sometimes dangerous. He can't spend his life living quietly at home with his immediate family, or the saving work would not get done.

Sometimes families have to share their loved ones with a wider circle of people, and Jesus wants to include as close family all those who are doing their best to live God's way. That is the 'family likeness' which marks many people out to be members of Jesus' family.

Things to discuss

1. It is quite an honour to be considered Jesus' close relatives! Do we behave as if this is true? Do we show any family likenesses?
2. What does it mean in practical terms to pray to God our Father: 'Let your will be done on earth as it is done in heaven'?

The Transfiguration

Thought for the day

In Jesus the full glory of God is revealed and encountered.

Things to read

Exodus 24:12-18
2 Peter 1:16-21
Matthew 17:1-9

Things to do

Aim: To see the meaning of the Transfiguration in the light of the Old Testament.

Show these pictures (or others of your own) which show only a small section of the complete object, and try to work out what the full pictures are.

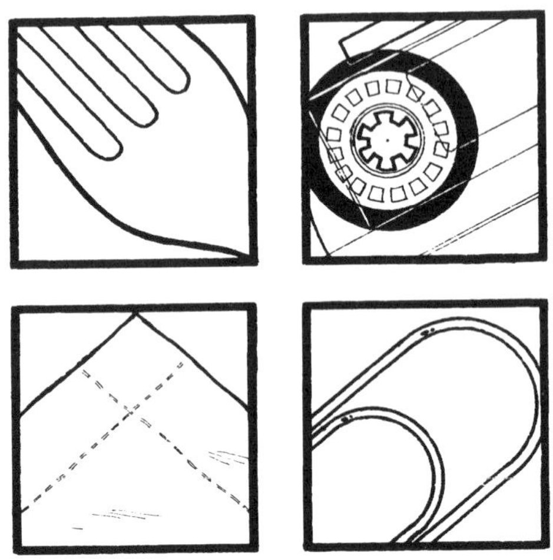

Have two large mountain shapes cut out of card or paper on which to record the details of the readings from Exodus 24 and Matthew 17. Read the first passage together and jot down all the points people have noticed, such as the name of the mountain, the names of those involved, and the signs of God's glory. Then read the Gospel together, and write down the salient facts on the other mountain shape. Place the two mountains side by side and talk about the similarities and differences.

Think about why Moses might be present at the Transfiguration, and also why Elijah is there. (They may need you to give a thumbnail sketch of the role of Moses and Elijah.) Help them to see that they represent the authority of the Law and the prophets, and see how this links in with the authority God's words give in declaring to the disciples who Jesus is.

Read 2 Peter 1:16-21 and discuss what the Transfiguration meant to Peter.

Things to discuss

1. Do we hit the right balance in our prayer and public worship between intimate friendship and awe in the presence of the almighty God?
2. Do we want to cling on to the 'mountain experiences' rather than accompany the living Jesus down to the demands of life in the valley?

Jesus Helps Us Start Again

Thought for the day

Jesus came to search out the lost and save them from the judgement of God.

Things to read

Isaiah 1:10-18
Psalm 32:1-7
Romans 2:1-11
Luke 19:1-10

Things to do

Aim: To see that Jesus enables us to make a fresh start when we have got our lives into a mess.

Play 'Twister', or make a long loop of string which everyone holds. When they have made themselves and the string loop into a muddle they sort themselves out, without letting go of the string.

Today we are going to look at how God helps us sort out our lives when we have got them into a mess. Start with the Isaiah reading, and work out why God is upset and hurt by their behaviour, when they are obviously all going along to services regularly.

Then read Psalm 32:1-7, as this is such an honest and helpful description of how it feels before and after admitting our fault. Perhaps they have already known it themselves.

Read the story of Zacchaeus, giving a few background details of how tax collectors were generally regarded and why. What might the people have been expecting Jesus to say to Zacchaeus in the tree? How would they have felt about his actual words, in view of his reputation? What do they think made Zacchaeus want to change his ways?

Look at Paul's letter to the Romans, chapter 2. Do we take seriously enough the fact that God will judge us, or do we tend to assume he'll let us off? Knowing there will be some kind of judgement, what do we need to sort out and change?

Things to discuss

1. Are we sometimes put off from making big, radical changes to our lifestyle or our giving in case we won't be able to cope? What does Zacchaeus' story say to us about such fears?
2. Is it better to avoid ritual completely in case it ever gets hypocritical and empty, or can it be useful in reminding us of our calling to holiness?

Jesus Rides To His Death

Thought for the day

As the Messiah, Jesus enters Jerusalem, knowing that he rides towards rejection and death in order to save his people.

Things to read

Isaiah 50:4-9a
Mark 14:1-15:47

Things to do

Gather all the age groups and take them on a Palm Sunday procession, preferably outside. Take a portable tape player so they can all sing along with the songs. The banners read 'Jesus is the Christ' and 'Jesus is the Messiah'.

Remind everyone of the way the prophets had known for many generations that God would one day send his chosen One, like a new King David, to save his people and reign for ever. The image they had of this Saviour was not all riding out to battle with the occupying army. Read from Isaiah 50, which is one of the passages about the suffering servant, noticing how the prophet senses the need for the Saviour to be despised and rejected as part of his saving work of love.

Notice the links with the story of the Passion, where we see Jesus in this suffering servant role. (Mark 14:1-15:47) Read the Passion with different voices for the different parts, with everyone reading the crowd parts. It is worthwhile to spend time on this.

Things to discuss

1. What do we discover about God's nature through the events of the Passion?
2. Why did the work of saving humanity have to end like this?

Christ Is Risen

Thought for the day

Jesus is alive; Love has won the victory over sin and death.

Things to read

Acts 10:34-43
John 20:1-18

Things to do

Spread out a whole pack of cards and ask one person to choose a card, without giving away which one is chosen. The rest of you are going to detect the right card by a process of elimination. The card chooser can only answer everyone's questions with a 'Yes' or 'No'. As each question is answered, turn over all the cards now eliminated, until the correct card is there, plain to see.

As we are used to celebrating Easter every year, the shock and impossibility of the event can get glossed over and taken for granted. As you read the Gospel account today, ask them to imagine they are particular characters (tell them which before you read) so that during the reading they are thinking through that person's head. Afterwards talk to everyone in character about how they felt, and how their feelings changed.

The reading from Acts will give extra insight into Peter's character, as this is his own later account of what happened, once he's had plenty of time to think things over. Has his conviction changed or is he still convinced that Jesus is alive?

Talk over the possibilities of what really happened. It's important that these are looked at and not assumed to be rubbish. Could Jesus have not really died, but just collapsed and later recovered? Could the disciples have stolen the body? Could the disciples and the women have wanted to see Jesus and so imagined they saw him?

Look at these questions in the light of the accounts they have read, so they can see that the strange truth is actually more likely. (*Who moved the stone?* by Frank Morison (Bromley, 1983) can be recommended for any wanting to read further.) The facts and circumstances point to Jesus dying and rising to new life. What does that say about who Jesus was? And is?

Things to discuss

1. What did the disciples gain from seeing Jesus after the Resurrection?

2. Since the Resurrection, Jesus is alive for all time, including today. Do we still tend to think of him in history? What evidence have we that Jesus is with us now?

On the Road with Jesus

Thought for the day

Jesus explains the scriptures and is recognised in the breaking of bread.

Things to read

Genesis 28:10-22
Luke 24:13-35

Things to do

Aim: To explore the Emmaus story and its relevance to our own journeys.

Pairs of shoes. Cut out a number of different-sized pairs of feet and mix them up. The group have to get them into pairs again, either with everyone being given a foot and trying to find the partner, or with all the feet displayed with letters and numbers around the room, so that the aim is to match number and letter correctly without actually touching any.

Today we are looking at a fourteen to sixteen mile walk, which took a lot longer going than coming back.

Read the passage from Luke together, with different people taking the speaking parts. Make a note of *who* is in the story, *where* it happened, *when* it happened and *what* took place. Sometimes it helps us to get down to practical details like this, and we notice things we may otherwise overlook. Suggest it as a useful way for them to think through their Bible-reading at home. Also look at possible *whys*. Why did Jesus appear to his disciples like this soon after the Resurrection? Was it for his benefit or theirs? What did he want them to understand about his risen life?

Now read the passage from Genesis. Can they see any links between the story of Jacob's journey and the disciples walking to Emmaus? In what ways are our own Christian journeys like theirs?

Things to discuss

1. Why didn't the disciples recognise Jesus at first?
2. Why did they recognise Jesus in the breaking of bread?

Thomas Finds Faith

Thought for the day

Step by step Thomas was led to believe in the risen Christ.

Things to read

Acts 4:32-35
John 20:19-31

Things to do

Give small groups clues to where the different components of a torch are. Each group races to be the first to assemble and light their torch. (Or you could have a tape player, lead, socket and tape to assemble.)

Our torches only lit up once we had gathered all the pieces and fitted them together. That's also how Inspector Morse or any other detective works. Our questions and investigations help us put facts and experiences together to reach a conclusion. Today we watch this happening in Thomas, one of the disciples who very much wanted to believe Jesus was risen, but found it very difficult. Read today's Gospel. Faced with the impossibility of death turning into risen life, what makes Thomas believe?

Working with the text, go through the stages:

1. For some reason Thomas was not with the others – denial and avoidance strategy.
2. Thomas hears the stories of the others – witnesses heard.
3. Can it be true? – wavers but digs in to avoid being conned and insists on solid evidence.
4. Thomas joins the disciples same place, same time, a week later – takes a risk and puts himself in right place just in case.
5. Meets Jesus – finds that the meeting is more convincing than anything, no more solid proof is needed.

Finally read the passage from Acts to hear the faith in action.

Things to discuss

1. Jesus breathes on his disciples the life which death cannot touch, the life of God's fullness. How does that change them?
2. What would you point to as evidence that Jesus is alive today, even though we cannot actually see him?

Different Routes to Faith

Thought for the day

Through the risen Jesus we have a living hope which will never spoil or fade.

Things to read

Acts 2:32-41
1 Corinthians 15:3-11
John 20

Things to do

Aim: To explore the way different people come to faith.

I know what this is, it's a . . . Pass around the group an ordinary object such as a sieve. Each person mimes a different way of using it. (For instance, someone might use it as a tennis racquet, someone else as a hat, and someone else as a ladle. The uses can be as ridiculous as they like.)

We are all different, and we all have different ways of doing things, as we have just seen! Today we are going to look at the different ways people were convinced that Jesus was alive again, and the different ways people find they come to faith today; there isn't just one way that is valid.

Have a sheet with the heading, 'Why I believe Jesus is alive', and look at the resurrection account in John 20. Go through some of the characters and as you mention them work together as a group to put into their words what seems to have clinched it for them (for example, Mary: 'I met him in the garden and he talked to me by name.') Look at Mary Magdalene, Peter and John and the other disciples in this way.

Now write up Thomas' name, and read together John 20:24-29. Why might Thomas not have been with the others on the first occasion? (We don't know, but it helps to imagine round the story.) Why might he have made sure he was there exactly a week later? What might he have been hoping? What might he have been dreading? What finally convinced Thomas? (Write this up with the others.)

Look at the passages from 1 Corinthians 15 and Acts 2 and ask how Paul and the early Christians came to believe in Jesus' resurrection, and record them on the chart.

Now look at all the reasons on the chart. Are there any reasons that are possible for us? (Believing what someone we trust has told us; meeting Jesus when we're together with other believers; meeting Jesus on our own when we are upset or in great need.) Point out that overwhelmingly it seems to be contact with the living person of Jesus that really convinces people, rather than argument and physical proof, though these certainly help to prepare us for believing. Add to the chart other reasons they have met (or known in their own experience) for people coming to a real faith (such as learning about Jesus at church, seeing Christian behaviour in their family and their upbringing, seeing the effects of unchristian behaviour in society).

Look again at the way Jesus recognises where Thomas is, and talks to him through it. That's what Jesus will always do. If we genuinely want to know the truth, he will help us to see it, starting from where we are and using our past experiences, both good and bad, in bringing us to faith along a path we can understand and manage to follow.

Things to discuss

1. How do you think you might have felt if you had been there that evening when Jesus appeared in the room? Does Jesus appear among us today?
2. Is there any way we can be sure that someone is speaking with God-given authority, rather than personal aggrandisement?

Glory and Suffering

Thought for the day

God's glory is often revealed in the context of suffering and failure in the world's eyes.

Things to read

Acts 1:6-14
1 Peter 4:12-14; 5:6-11
John 17:1-11

Things to do

Aim: To explore the nature of Jesus' glory both on the cross and in heaven.

Make some rubbings of various coins, from different countries, a heads and a tails rubbing for each coin.

The two sides of a coin both belong equally to the coin, but show us completely different faces of it; and today we are going to look at something which at first sight seems like two different things, but which is actually two sides of the same coin.

First read the account in Acts of the Ascension. Place on the floor a large cross cut out of dark-coloured sugar paper, and chalks to record ideas on it, and also a large sun shape with zigzag edges cut out of sunny-coloured sugar paper, and crayons to record ideas. Explain that one of the things we are looking at is the cross of Christ, and the other is Christ in glory, having ascended into heaven as a hero. Ask the group to write on the two shapes any words or phrases which come to mind about these two things.

Share what has been suggested in each case, and you will find that they are much more closely linked than you might expect. Read together John 17:1-11, and relate it to your findings recorded on the cross and glory symbols. The Ascension brings us to a place where heaven and earth meet and overlap for a while (overlap the two symbols).

Then read the passage from 1 Peter 4, and listen out for any overlapping of the cross and the glory in that.

To express something of this mystery, suggest they create a picture which shows the Ascension from two angles at once – from the earthly and the heavenly viewpoint. They can use symbols and colours, and make the dividing line clear, or mingle the two 'planes'.

Things to discuss

1. What do you think the disciples had to learn about Jesus, between the Resurrection and the Ascension?
2. Is our society so frightened by suffering, and so bent on avoiding it, that we can no longer appreciate the way it can show us God's glory?

Christ the King

Thought for the day

Jesus Christ is the everlasting King whose kingdom is not of this world, but grows in the hearts of his people and lasts for ever.

Things to read

Daniel 7:9-10, 13-14
Revelation 1:4b-8
John 18:33-37

Things to do

Give everyone a large post-it note on which they write ten sentences beginning with 'I am . . .' Then they stick their note to themselves and go round reading one another's statements.

It's not easy to decide on ten 'I am . . .' statements, but taken altogether they do give a little idea of who we are. Today we are in a way summing up everything we know about Jesus Christ, both on earth and in heaven, and the shorthand for all of that is that he is Christ the King. We'll try to unpack it a bit.

Begin by reading Daniel's vision. It's obviously impossible to describe heaven exactly, but look at the images and talk over what they say to us. Also point out that Daniel was writing long before Jesus had come, yet he 'sees' Jesus entering heaven and being made king.

Now go to the Gospel, reading it with different people taking the different parts. Pilate's job, as Roman governor, is to establish whether this so-called king is likely to pose a threat to the Roman empire. As Jesus says, that would be so if his kingdom were 'of this world'. But it isn't. In what way is the kingdom of heaven not 'of this world'? If the territory of the kingdom of heaven is not geographical, where is it found? (Think back to the parables of the kingdom, and all Jesus' teaching about kingdom living.)

So today we see Jesus entering heaven in glory, and at his most weak and vulnerable, humanly speaking, on earth. All of that is the same Jesus, the Servant King who was obedient even to death on a cross.

Finally look at the reading from Revelation, where Jesus Christ is seen as the faithful witness, the firstborn from the dead, and the ruler of the kings of the earth.

We are reminded that Jesus is the visible image of the unseen God, totally faithful to speaking out God's words and revealing his love to us. And one day he will come in glory, seen by everybody.

As we consider all we have learnt of Jesus, it makes us want to worship, and proclaim with Christians all over the world and all through history, that Jesus Christ is Lord!

Things to discuss

1. How does this faith we celebrate today transform our outlook and enable us to face suffering?
2. What is your vision of heaven?

God's People

Friends of Jesus

Thought for the day

If we are Jesus' friends we will love one another as Jesus loves us.

Things to read

1 John 4:7-12
John 15:9-15

Things to do

Act out the following sketches.

The Servant

The employer is talking on his mobile phone, pacing up and down, with a file open. He's sorting out some complex problem. The office cleaner comes in with feather duster and starts cleaning.

Mr King *(Into phone)* Quite . . . Quite . . . But look at these figures on page 24 . . . *(catches sight of Marg the cleaner)* Marg, get me a strong coffee. And a doughnut or something. *(Returns to phone)* Yes, these figures should have warned us . . . Well, the point is, what can we do about it now?

(Marg reappears with coffee and doughnut.)

Marg Coffee, Mr King. It's strong. And a doughnut. *(Puts them on desk)*

Mr King *(Still on phone, listening and making 'mm' noises. Motions with hand for Marg not to interrupt him as he's busy.)* Sorry, Steve, say that again . . . the schedules systematically reduced what? . . . Oh, I see. Yes, of course. So what are you going to do about it?

(Marg continues dusting.)

Mr King *(Still on phone)* Marg, get me the February file – it's there on my desk. *(Talks into phone)* It seems to me we can possibly get ourselves out of this mess, Steve. I've just had an idea.

(Marg brings the February file to Mr King.)

Marg The February file, Mr King.

Mr King *(Takes it without thanking her and starts looking in it. Into phone he says)* Yes, here it is! I'm looking at these figures for the second week of February . . .

(Marg goes back to the dusting. The desk phone rings.)

Mr King Answer that, Marg.

Marg *(Picks up phone)* Hello, Mr King's office. Well, he's very busy at the moment, in an important meeting . . . Oh, I've no idea, I'm only the cleaner here. I just do what I'm told.

The Friends

Norman and Pete walk up to a bench and sit down. They put their rucksacks down.

Pete Phew! That was quite a climb, wasn't it. What a view, though, eh?

Norman Marvellous, isn't it. *(Pause)* Anyway, you were saying about your interview . . .

Pete Oh yeah, that's right. So we've got to decide whether to move or not, basically. And that's a big decision to make.

Norman How does Sheila feel about moving? She's settled here, isn't she?

Pete Yes, it would be quite a wrench for her, but you know Sheila, she's willing to give it a go if she feels it's what God wants for us.

Norman Funny, isn't it. This time last year, there you were just made redundant, no hopes for the future, and now this new door seems to be opening for you. I'm happy for you, Pete.

Pete Thanks, Norman. Well, you've been a good friend through all this – it's always good to talk things over with you. Shall we be on our way then? *(They get up and walk off.)*

All four characters I no longer call you servants, because a servant doesn't know his master's business. Instead I have called you friends.

Now look at 1 John 4:7-12 and John 15:9-15. Make it clear that we are not obeying his commands in order for him to like us. It's God's love for us which makes us love him and want to be his friends.

Things to discuss

Imagine walking through a normal day, meeting the usual people and problems, but in the knowledge of God's love and forgiveness, and literally loving as Jesus loves us. What would it be like, and how would it differ from how we usually live?

Called to Serve

Thought for the day

When God calls us to serve him we have to trust him to equip us for the task.

Things to read

Jonah 3:1-5, 10
Mark 1:14-20

Things to do

Give out a circled job advertisement in a newspaper, and prepare three or four simple profiles to give the applicants, including such facts as age, qualifications and experience. The rest of the group are the panel interviewing them for the job, and they decide which one to appoint.

When God calls people for particular jobs, he already knows all about them, and knows they will be perfectly suited to the work he is calling them to. (That's why it's such a sensible idea to consult God when we are thinking about jobs we might do.) But when God calls, it doesn't always look like what we were hoping to do.

Read the passage from Jonah, reminding them of what had happened the first time God wanted Jonah to call the citizens of Nineveh to repentance. In today's passage we find Jonah being obedient to his call, and the people are also obedient to their calling; they decide to reject their evil ways and turn back to God. God knew that Jonah was the right person for the job, but he could only use him if Jonah willingly agreed. All kinds of good doesn't get done because the people God wants to call aren't listening.

Now look at the calling of the first disciples in today's Gospel. These four people hear the call and respond to it straightaway. Something in Jesus makes them sure that this wild and crazy idea of following a wandering preacher is a good one, if unusual and unexpected. They can feel how important it is, even though they don't yet know exactly why.

When God calls us, he doesn't lay all the details out straightaway. He just lodges the conviction in us that we have to follow him in a particular direction, and as we start to follow, the next bit of the job becomes clearer. He never forces or pressurises us, though if, like Jonah, we start haring off in the other direction, he'll wait to get our attention again and then quietly repeat the same call. If we agree to follow, he'll set off and expect us to keep up with him. The fishermen were probably surprised it happened to be they who were called; we shouldn't be too surprised if we find God calling us!

Things to discuss

1. Are there occasions when we sense God's call and direction but fail to run with it in case we are mistaken?
2. What makes people able to understand and respond to God's call and what hinders them?

Called to be Saints

Thought for the day

Lives that have shone with God's love on earth are filled with joy as they see their Lord face to face.

Things to read

1 John 3:1-3
Matthew 5:1-12
Revelation 7:9-17

Things to do

Aim: To explore sanctity and the heavenly reward.

Provide each group with a diary or prayerbook which gives saints' days, together with a book of saints to use as a reference book. Give each group a list of dates, and they have to discover whose saints' days these are, and what each saint is remembered for. Here are some dates to choose from:

- 1 March: Saint David
- 17 March: Saint Patrick
- 23 April: Saint George
- 19 May: Saint Dunstan
- 9 June: Saint Columba
- 22 June: Saint Alban
- 11 August: Saint Clare
- 27 August: Saint Monica
- 17 September: Saint Hildegard
- 4 October: Saint Francis
- 11 November: Saint Martin
- 16 November: Saint Margaret, Queen of Scotland
- 30 November: Saint Andrew
- 6 December: Saint Nicholas
- 26 December: Saint Stephen

Then they can tell one another what they've discovered.

All through the year we celebrate the saints, and today we remember all of them, together with all those unknown to us but known to God for their special friendship. What is saintliness? Is it a demure, holy expression on a painting or in a stained-glass window? No. They are ordinary people, made extraordinary by their openness to God and their dependence on him.

Read the Gospel passage, preferably in a translation which is accessible to their understanding. These 'Beatitudes' or the 'blesseds' are aptly named, since they do stress the natural happy outcome of living in the way of God's love. It is knowing our need of God that opens us up to receive all the gifts he longs to give us. The Beatitudes are like the saintly handbook.

1 John 3:1-3 looks forward to the hope which is seen in the vision of Revelation 7. Explain the difficulties of expressing heaven in images of time and human experience, and list the qualities of heaven that this passage hints at.

Things to discuss

1. What factors prevent us loving God with all our hearts?
2. What prevents us from trusting God with our deepest needs?

Responding to God's Call

Thought for the day

Jesus came from God to call us to follow him.

Things to read

1 Samuel 3:1-10 (11-20)
John 1:43-51

Things to do

One person tries to keep a completely still face, without responding to the others at all. They try their best to make the person laugh, but they can only use their voices (no tickling allowed).

Sometimes we don't respond or answer when we're called, especially if we don't want to hear what we think someone is going to ask us! Other times, we're sitting waiting to be called and jump up to respond as soon as possible. Today we are going to look at people who are called and respond.

First read the passage from 1 Samuel, talking about the way Samuel heard God's call even before he realised it was possible for God to get in touch with him, and what he heard put him in the tricky position of having to give unpleasant and scary news to his guardian. God needed this young boy to do a particular job.

Today's Gospel shows us Jesus calling some of his disciples from their ordinary lives to take part in the extraordinary work of accompanying the Son of God on his rescue mission of love. How do Philip and Nathanael respond? Philip immediately goes off to tell Nathanael about Jesus – he's bursting with the news. Nathanael is at first sceptical, but Jesus' knowledge of him convinces him that this person is worth cancelling everything for.

Things to discuss

1. Do you think God calls us to do particular jobs which only we can do? What might they be?
2. If Jesus Christ is the one who reveals and makes clear the hiddenness of God, what does that suggest the Church should be doing – and are we doing it?

Bearing Fruit

Thought for the day

To produce fruit we need to be joined on to the true vine.

Things to read

Acts 8:26-40
John 15:1-8

Things to do

Provide a length of wire, a torch battery and bulb, and make the bulb light up.

Read the passage from Acts together, looking at the stages Philip goes through with the Ethiopian, which link up once again with Jesus' example:

- listening expectantly to God and co-operating right away
- listening to where the Ethiopian is spiritually at the moment
- answering the Ethiopian's questions
- leading him on from here using the scriptures with which he is familiar
- helping him see the truth about Jesus

And this is a very good model for all of us when spreading the good news.

Philip was producing a rich harvest of spiritual fruit, and he was able to because he was constantly connected to Jesus. Jesus had talked about how important this was in the Gospel for today. Read this now.

How can we make sure we are part of the true vine? Look at being baptised, daily prayer and Bible reading, coming to worship regularly with the other people of God, and committing our life direction to match up with the will of God.

Things to discuss

1. How can we check that we are still firmly attached to the true vine?
2. Does belonging to the true vine mean that we have to sacrifice our independence?

The Guidance of the Holy Spirit

Thought for the day

The continuing presence of God, as Holy Spirit, leads us, as Jesus promised, into new areas of life and discipleship.

Things to read

Proverbs 16:1-3, 9; 19:21
Acts 16:6-15
John 14:25-26; 16:12-15

Things to do

Aim: To explore the nature of the guiding of the Holy Spirit.

Borrow a game of Mastermind, or look at an adventure game book, where you are gradually guided to the correct solution by various clues and choices.

Point out that in the game you worked in partnership with the feedback to reach the solution, though all the time you were free to take the advice or ignore it. Today we are looking at the help Jesus promised would be available to all his friends, including us, when he was no longer walking physically around the planet. Read the verses from John 14 and 16 to see what Jesus said about this help.

Now look at an example of it working out in practice. I suggest you read Acts 16, starting back at verse 6 to see how things didn't go the way they expected. If you have a map of the Mediterranean you can track their route. Read as far as verse 8 first, and talk together about times we have had plans, both as individuals and as a Church, and we seem to be blocked all the time. It may be that in these blockings God is allowing time for a better plan to become possible. It is very important that praying Christians of all ages know this.

Then read on to verse 10, noting how God will make it quite clear if there is a particular course of action that needs to be taken, and we are always left free to take the advice or ignore it. The Spirit leads, but never shoves. Finally read the rest of the passage, where the needs are drawn together with those who can help, and as a result, a new Church is started.

Things to discuss

1. Share any experiences you have had of being led in unexpected ways in directions which have turned out to be valuable.
2. Do we pray for guidance out of habit, or are we aware of the real openings it can put before us.

Good Leadership

Thought for the day

Jesus' caring ministry is a good example for all Christian leaders.

Things to read

Jeremiah 23:1-6
Mark 6:30-34, 53-56

Things to do

What's my line? Take it in turns to mime a job while the others try to work out what that job is.

Begin by reading what God thought of the job being done by the leaders of his people during the time of Jeremiah, not long before they were taken off into Babylon as exiles. Note the reasons why God is going to punish these irresponsible leaders. Also draw attention to the love God has for his people as he talks of a future leader who will take proper care of them. That would be quite a job, and only one person could do it.

Look next at the Gospel to see Jesus in action. Jot down what everyone notices about his ministry, as if you are compiling a job description. (For example: on call 24 hours a day; no guaranteed regular holiday; accommodation and food variable according to availability and others' hospitality; salary £00.00. Highly demanding but highly rewarding work.)

Encourage them to imagine what such a ministry would feel like as a disciple, as Jesus himself, and as someone among the crowds.

Things to discuss

1. Jesus tried to ensure that his disciples had times of rest and spiritual refreshment. Do we follow that example in our church community?

2. Why were the crowds going out of their way to flock to Jesus?

Good News

Thought for the day

The good news about God is far too good to keep to ourselves.

Things to read

1 Corinthians 9:16-23
Mark 1:29-39

Things to do

Have a selection of newspaper headlines and stories. These are to be sorted into different categories:

- Gossip
- The odd/unusual
- Important good news
- Important bad news

Leading on from this, talk together about what we consider is news worth spreading around in our newspapers each day. Notice which kind of stories are considered most newsworthy, and whether good news is considered worth printing. If they were to become an editor, would they want to change what is thought worth spreading?

Now read today's Gospel, looking at why Jesus wants to move on from Capernaum. What is it that he has seen in the eyes of those he has healed which makes him anxious to spread the good news as widely as possible? (Such things as joy and freedom from pain or guilt; they look as if they have just been set free.) The news we have to tell about Jesus is worth telling because lives can be set free as a result of knowing it. People surely have a right to know something that has the power to change their lives for the better.

Read the passage from 1 Corinthians to see how, for Paul, too, telling people about God's real power and presence is an urgent matter – he can't bear for anyone to be left without the opportunity to know God and benefit from his saving love.

Things to discuss

1. What would you most want people to know about God?
2. What do you think is the best way of telling them?

The Saints in Heaven

Thought for the day

Great is the rejoicing in heaven among the saints of God as they worship their Lord in glory.

Things to read

Isaiah 25:6-9
Psalm 24:1-6
Revelation 21:1-6a

Things to do

Give one person a painting of heaven as painted by an artist (a print such as you find on some Christmas cards, where heaven is visible above the stable; or in an art book). Without the others seeing the picture, the person describes it to them in detail, and they imagine it. Then everyone is shown the actual picture. How is it like they imagined, and how is it completely different?

Today we are celebrating all the lives well lived and shining with God's love. Anyone who has continued faithfully on their journey through life, close to God and ready to work with him, will be among those living for ever in the joy of heaven. The reading from Psalm 24 celebrates those who are eligible. (What does the psalmist mean by having clean hands and a pure heart?)

Now read the passage from Revelation, which picks up on the Isaiah reading. The writer is describing the welcome into heaven in picture language.

Encourage them to describe heaven in their own way, in pictures or in words.

Things to discuss

1. If your life was in a book of saints, what would you like it to say about you?
2. Which saint do you particularly admire and why?

Lord of all Nations (1)

Thought for the day

Jesus, the promised Messiah, is shown to the Gentile world.

Things to read

Isaiah 60:1-6
Ephesians 3:5-11
Matthew 2:1-12

Things to do

In a circle, pass a bus or train ticket around, and each person in turn says how they got here today. Then pass a cross around. Each person says how they're a Christian, or where they feel they are, how they got here and who has helped them on the way. (As with all circle time, those who don't wish to speak can pass the cross on, and it's fine to say the same as someone else has said if their situation is the same.)

Then read today's Gospel reading, establishing what we know from the account about where the wise men came from, how many and who they were. Draw attention to their not being Jewish, but pagan foreigners. Imagine together some of the dangers they may have faced on their journey. Why were they wanting to bother with it? How was the king they found different from what they were expecting?

Now look at Ephesians 3, reading verses 5-11, so they can see how Paul's calling was carrying on the mission to spread the good news to all the non-Jewish people, including us, if we are Gentiles. Finally look at Isaiah 60 to see how this had been prophesied generations before.

Make a banner or poster which expresses our many different journeys to Christ, who welcomes us wherever we have come from.

Things to discuss

1. Why do you think Matthew, writing for the Hebrew people, considered this event of the wise men's visit so important to include?
2. What can we, both as Gentiles and as members of the Church, learn from the Magi's visit about our own attitudes and calling?

Lord of all Nations (2)

Thought for the day

Through Christ's death, full life would come to people of all nations and generations.

Things to read

Isaiah 49:1-6
John 12:20-33

Things to do

Have some blotting paper and dampen it so they can watch a blob of colour from various dark-coloured felt-tip pens spreading out in all directions and revealing lots of hidden colours.

Have the spreading blots displayed as you read the passage from Isaiah, focusing on verse 6. Go on to look at John 12:20-22. As this Gospel is very condensed, it's best to take it in sections.

Explain that the Greeks were Gentiles, and John wants us to know that here are representatives from the 'other nations' seeking Jesus out. Take them briefly back to the wedding at Cana (John 2:3-5) where Jesus had said his hour had not yet come, and then read what Jesus says when he finds these Gentiles looking for him (John 12:23). Everyone can read this verse aloud together. This is the point in Jesus' ministry when the 'standby for action' lights start flashing. The big act of total self-giving has moved from the long-term planning stage to red alert, and, humanly speaking, Jesus' adrenaline starts pumping.

As he starts teaching them about what to expect (John 12:24-26) all the horror of what it will entail rushes in to him, and John gives us a blow-by-blow account of Jesus, the Son of God, wrestling with the human temptation to scream, 'Stop! I can't go through with it!' (verse 27). What will happen? Wonderfully, Jesus manages to triumph in that battle, and chooses for God's name to be glorified, whatever the cost to himself (verse 28a).

We can imagine God the Father on the edge of his seat (so to speak) through Jesus' agonising, and now immediately he is there to affirm and comfort him, giving him a new surge of confidence, which we can hear in Jesus' voice in the last couple of verses (28b-33).

Things to discuss

1. How does it help that even Jesus shrank from the thought of the suffering ahead?
2. How is it that Jesus being lifted up (both when crucified and ascended) can draw all humanity to himself?

God's Way

Finding God's Way

Thought for the day

After his Baptism Jesus is led by the Spirit into the wilderness before returning to proclaim God's kingdom.

Things to read

Psalm 25:4-10
Mark 1:9-15

Things to do

Set up a short orienteering course, with something to collect from each point as they reach it. You will need to make a chart of the area on squared paper, marking the squares with numbers and letters (as shown below) so that they can find their way by map co-ordinates.

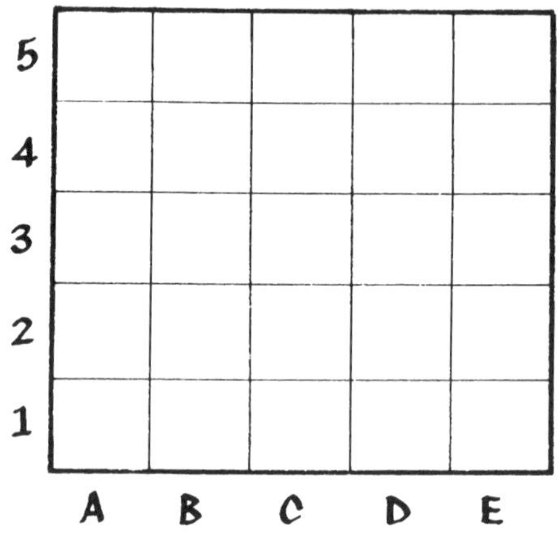

Going through life is rather like finding our way through a landscape, and we need maps and a compass to guide us. Jesus referred to himself as the Way, which we can follow and trust. But, before he was able to start on that ministry, he had some working out to do himself.

Read the Gospel for today. What happened straight after Jesus had been baptised? Did he start his work immediately? No, he went out into the loneliness and discipline of the desert for forty days to search out what his role was, and how he needed to be spending the rest of his life on earth. It was a time of severe and difficult testing, which he had to go through, keeping to the right direction by keeping close to God and his word in scripture, as the doubts and temptations battled in him.

Only then could he come back into circulation and

start his life's work. What are we told his work was? Proclaiming that God's kingdom is very near.

Lent gives us a chance to spend the same amount of time as Jesus spent in the desert, facing ourselves and our commitment to living God's way; to live more simply and rigorously while we allow God to prepare us for our own ministry as baptised Christians, proclaiming the risen Christ. It's all carefully thought out that Easter, the festival celebrating Christ's Resurrection, follows straight on from this 'desert season' of Lent.

Things to discuss

1. Why can God only work with us in earnest when we are totally honest with him?
2. What is it that makes us decide whether or not discipleship is too costly?

Jesus Shows Us the Way

Thought for the day

Jesus is the Way, the Truth and the Life, through whom we can come into the presence of God for ever.

Things to read

Acts 7:54-60
John 14:1-14

Things to do

Aim: To see Jesus as the Way, the Truth and the Life.

Using some road maps, give each couple of people a destination and a place to set out from. They have to work out the best route to take. Share their recommendations.

Point out that although they may never have been somewhere, it is still quite easy to get there, providing you know the way. That's why the AA make all these maps! They recognise that if we didn't know the way, we'd all get hopelessly lost and they'd have to keep coming out to rescue stranded motorists. Today we find Jesus talking to his friends, who are very worried about the future. They know that their leader is in great danger, and they don't really know what is going to happen, or how they are going to be able to cope. It's like lots of us feel at some points in our life. There is confusion, anxiety, and insecurity about the future, and how we will cope.

We are going to find out what Jesus has to offer to anyone in that situation. Read together John 14:1-6. Draw out the lovely reassurance that Jesus gives, and the way he understands how the disciples are feeling, and doesn't tell them to pull themselves together, but gives them a promise that he is going to provide for them personally. Their relationship with him will be like a clear road to walk along which will bring them safely through every danger to heaven.

Now read on to verse 10. Philip (and perhaps the others as well) still doesn't understand that Jesus is the way we are able to see God. We wouldn't be able, as humans, to cope with seeing the full glory of God without it being acted out in a human life – which is why Jesus was born as a human baby.

Next read the passage from Acts, to see that Way in action. Even when Stephen is having his life smashed out of him with stones, he is still aware of the close presence of Jesus, and that way of loving forgiveness and truth is what is keeping Stephen safe, in terms of everlasting life, right through all his troubles, including torture and death.

Things to discuss

1. Why are we sometimes more inclined to go for a code of rules than a personal relationship with the living God?
2. We are told that Saul was minding the coats of those stoning Stephen to death for blasphemy. How might he have viewed what Stephen said, both at the time and after his Damascus road experience?

Hearing and Believing

Thought for the day

If we are not ready to listen to the truth, we will not hear it.

Things to read

Ezekiel 2:1-5
Mark 6:1-13

Things to do

Play 'pick-up-sticks', either with a commercial set, or by tipping a pile of cutlery on to the table and taking it in turns to lift off one item at a time very carefully, so as not to wobble the rest.

That was a bit how it feels to be talking about our faith to someone who is determined not to believe a word of what we're saying! We have to go very carefully and sensitively, looking out for where those people are coming from, so we can talk into their questions and help them understand. Today we are reading about the way the people in Jesus' home town reacted to him. Read Mark 6:1-6 and look out for why they rejected him.

However, there were huge numbers of people living in the area who needed to be told the good news, so this is how Jesus decided to reach those people. Read Mark 6:7-13 and look out for the instructions Jesus gave his disciples as he sent them off. They are to do with travelling light, living simply and involving the community.

Now read the passage from Ezekiel, where the prophet is told to tell out God's words, even though he knows there will be many who refuse to listen. Talk together about our own lives and the people we know. How are they to be told about the God who made them and longs for them to live freely in his forgiving love, instead of living just for material things and personal comfort?

Pray for one another in the group about particular situations that come up in the conversation, and particular people they want to help hear God's message.

Things to discuss

1. How genuinely receptive are we to God's word? Do we mark out 'no-go' areas where God is concerned?
2. How might our gut reactions alert us to God trying to tell us something important, which we don't really want to hear?

Obeying God's Rules

Thought for the day

God's wisdom may shock us. Jesus, obedient to God's Law and fulfilling it, dies a death which, according to the Law, makes him cursed.

Things to read

Exodus 20:1-17
John 2:13-22

Things to do

They invent a simple ball game with clear rules, which gives everyone a chance to be involved.

Point out the value of the rules, which make it possible for the game to be played and uphold fair play. Before you read the ten commandments from Exodus, check that they remember who is being given these rules and when. (The people of Israel, through their leader, Moses, after they had escaped from slavery in Egypt and were wandering in the wilderness.)

As each of the commandments is read (reading around the group), place cards of individual commandments on the table, together with memory joggers as follows: a large number one; a blank piece of paper; a cardboard speech bubble with 'Keep It Clean' written on it; a calendar page with Sunday circled in red; a bunch of flowers with a label reading 'To Mum and Dad'; a gun; a wedding congratulations card; a swag bag; a file clearly labelled 'Lies'; and a thought bubble with 'If only . . .' written on it.

Draw attention to the first commandment, and discuss what they might expect God's temple to be like, in the light of this rule. You could also refer to Isaiah 56:7. Bearing those ideas in mind, read the Gospel for today, so they can see how far the people had wandered from God's will as expressed in that first commandment.

How was Jesus being obedient to God's Law? When might obedience to God mean getting into trouble with the Law?

Things to discuss

1. In what way is the 'Law of the Lord' refreshing to us, reviving the spirit?
2. What was it about the temple that made Jesus so angry? Might he find anything in our churches to anger him?

Loving Obedience

Thought for the day

Loving obedience to God is shown by Jesus to be a quality rich in courage and wisdom, a quality to be highly respected and imitated.

Things to read

Isaiah 50:4-9a
Mark 8:27-38

Things to do

Collect some snails and stage a snail race down a pre-marked sheet of A4 paper.

However much we shouted encouragement at our snails, they weren't able to be particularly obedient either to us, or to the ruled lines marking their lanes. They still have no idea of what they were supposed to be doing. Today we are going to look at what obedience really is.

Begin by reading the passage from Isaiah 50, describing God's obedient Servant, willing to go along with God's guidance even in the face of violent opposition. Who does it sound like? For us, living after Jesus' coming, the passage points very significantly to Jesus, describing the kind of loving obedience he showed during all his life and particularly in his trial and crucifixion. This kind of obedience came from the way Jesus was always so close to his Father – at one with him, so that God's will was also Jesus' will.

Now look at today's Gospel from Mark 8. Jesus is making it plain that part of being the Christ is the necessity to go through the suffering foretold by the prophets. That loving obedience is all part of Jesus' identity as the Messiah, or holy, anointed One of God. And Jesus goes further; it's also part of being someone who claims to be one of Christ's followers, like us. If we mean what we say, it will involve a daily willingness to walk the way of the cross (verse 34).

Have the words of the Lord's Prayer available, and draw their attention to the way the first section of the prayer is placing ourselves in that loving obedience, whenever we say, 'Let your kingdom come; let your will be done on earth as it is in heaven.' Do we realise what we are saying here? We need to do that conscious placing of ourselves in obedience to God every single time we say those words – and say them at least morning, afternoon and evening every day.

Things to discuss

1. Has the time come to take another look at obedience and see if we've grown up enough to consider it a Godly quality worth developing?
2. Why does Jesus say that following him is bound to involve taking up our cross as he did?

True Greatness

Thought for the day

The truly great in God's eyes are those who are prepared to be last of all and servant of all.

Things to read

Philippians 2:1-11
Mark 9:30-37

Things to do

Have a number of pictures of famous people from newspapers and magazines cut out and stuck around the room, numbered. Give out sheets of paper. Everyone goes round writing down the names of those pictured. The one with most right gets to wear a posh hat to show how clever they are.

All the people in those pictures were famous, for all sorts of reasons. They were all 'the greatest' in their particular area. Now read today's Gospel, where the disciples have been arguing about which of them should be the greatest. Why were they ashamed to admit to Jesus what they had been talking about? Why might their argument have disturbed Jesus? (He knew that they were going to be the leaders of the Church, and here they were behaving like pagan leaders, full of boasting and jealousy.) Notice how Jesus both explains and shows them, with the little child, what he means. Children were vulnerable, and with no status at all, so to accept Jesus by accepting them suggests that he is prepared to think of himself on a level with what most people would consider the very lowest of the low. (How do we choose our friends? Would we feel embarrassed to be seen with some people because our other friends despise them?)

Now read the passage from Philippians, noting that boasting and selfishness have no place in the Christian life. Our greatest example of humility and self-giving is Jesus Christ himself.

Things to discuss

1. How much does the Church look as if it is based on the principle of the greatest being the last and the servant of all? Does anything need changing?
2. What kind of ambition is appropriate for followers of Jesus?

That Sinking Feeling

Thought for the day

God is faithful to us through all the storms of life, yet our faith in God is so very small.

Things to read

1 Kings 19:9-18
Psalm 69:1-3
Matthew 14:22-33

Things to do

Aim: To look at that sinking feeling, and Jesus' rescue.

Provide some bowls of water and see how much cargo floating tubs can hold before they sink. This could be done in two teams, to see whose boat stays afloat longest.

First today we are looking at a prophet with that sinking feeling. It's Elijah, who has done wonderful things which witness to the truth of the living God, and is at present exhausted and dejected and fearful. Read 1 Kings 19:9-18, imagining how Elijah might have felt when at last he knew God's presence in the still small whisper.

Now look at Matthew 14:22-33, jotting down the details under the following headings: Who? Where? When? What? How? Then think about 'why?' (What did Peter and the others learn from the incident? What new light does it throw on Jesus' identity?) Draw attention to the way you can often do things you would think impossible if you are following the instructions of a dynamic teacher or instructor. (Think of those TV documentaries about scary rescues, where ordinary passengers need to take over the flight controls and are talked safely down to landing by trusting the instructor in the control tower enough to do exactly as they say.) Jesus sees it all as a question of faith – the sort of faith which would make us quite naturally take an umbrella with us to pray for rain. This sort of faith expects real results, and, says Jesus, the results will happen. It's often our lack of real, practical believing in God which prevents his work from happening.

Things to discuss

1. What kind of things build up our faith, and what knocks it about?
2. What can we learn from Elijah and Peter about God's reaction to people at the low and vulnerable points of life?

Trust in God

Thought for the day

A commitment of faith has far-reaching implications.

Things to read

Genesis 17:1-7, 15-16
Romans 4:13-25
Mark 8:31-38

Things to do

Blindfold everyone securely and lead them in a line through doorways and up stairs, quietly giving guidance to the one immediately next to you, so they all start warning one another of hazards approaching, and are therefore developing group trust.

The blindfolds make us all more vulnerable, so we have to start looking after one another and our trust in one another grows. Sometimes we go through dark times in life, but we can trust God right through them. Read the passage from Genesis to see how Abraham was willing to go on trusting in God, even when there didn't seem to be much chance of God's promise coming true. Then read Romans 4, where Paul sees all those who stick with God in faith as being the real descendants of Abraham, including the Gentiles – including us!

Jesus wanted to prepare his disciples for a very dark time ahead, when he knew their faith would be shaken. It is quite typical of God to prepare us before some severe time of testing. Read the Gospel to find out how Jesus honestly and openly tells his followers what to expect, and still promises that if they stay firm, all will be well.

Things to discuss

1. In what sense are we descendants of Abraham?
2. Why is it that living God's way of love inevitably leads us into conflict?

Facing Persecution

Thought for the day

Those who speak out God's will are bound to be vulnerable to rejection and abuse.

Things to read

Amos 7:7-15
1 Peter 3:8-17
Mark 6:14-29

Things to do

Tie a length of string across the room at just above head height and provide two different coloured balloons. Split the group either side of the string, each with a balloon. Both sides aim to get their balloon to touch the floor on the other side, while preventing the other balloon from coming to land on their own side.

Draw attention to the way we all did our best to hit that approaching balloon back where it came from. We do just the same in arguments. If someone says something about us that we don't want to hear, we hit it back as fast as we can. Today we are reading about the way prophets are treated when they go on speaking out God's words which people don't want to hear.

Read the Amos passage, noticing how faithfulness to God is despised and rejected. Then read today's Gospel, where John the Baptist is hated and eventually put to death because the words of God which he insists on speaking out are uncomfortable for Herodias to hear. Suppose instead of shutting her ears to what John was saying, she and Herod had listened. What might have happened?

When we shut our ears to hearing what God wants us to know, we shut out all kinds of possible good in our lives, and open up all kinds of possibilities of evil.

Finally look at 1 Peter 3:8-17 and note that even if we face opposition we should remain calm and not react angrily or aggressively. Note especially verses 15 and 16.

Things to discuss

1. How ready are we to speak out God's truth and God's values when we know they will make us unpopular?
2. How can we best support and encourage the young people as they live and work in environments often openly hostile to God?

God's Wisdom

Thought for the day

God's wisdom may appear foolishness without the God-given grace to understand.

Things to read

Proverbs 9:1-6
1 Corinthians 1:18-25
John 6:51-69

Things to do

Sing one of those silly songs with actions, such as 'Did you ever see a zombie come to tea? Take a look at me – a zombie you will see.' With each verse an extra action is added: marching with feet, right arm up and down, left arm up and down, nod head, blink.

Now we have all made ourselves look ridiculous! Today we are going to look at how God's wisdom is often seen as complete foolishness. Perhaps they have already been made to feel foolish for believing in God and talking to him. It is never a nice experience, and can set us wondering why we bother with God if it's going to make some people laugh at us and think we're stupid. (Of course, God is there whether we bother with him or not, so it won't make God disappear if we deny him. Nor will it help those who are doing the scoffing. But we do need to support one another with our prayers, and to know that Jesus received the same scorn from his contemporaries.)

Read the passage from Proverbs, telling them also about the lady Folly, in contrast to Wisdom. At first sight Folly can look like a good idea, appealing to our instincts and cravings, rather like much of the media does today. Only after people have made their choice is it clear that this leads to death, whereas the path of Wisdom leads to life-giving nourishment and fulfilment.

Now look at today's Gospel, where the religious leaders, and even some of Jesus' own followers, are finding it impossible to see his words as wisdom, but only as foolishness and blasphemy. What stops them seeing the truth of Jesus' words? (Look at their expectations of the Messiah, their attention to precise detail at the expense of the wider vision, and their status as learned, respected leaders in the community.)

Things to discuss

1. What is the difference between being clever, learned and knowledgeable, and being wise?
2. Why do learned and clever people often find it harder to understand God's wisdom? (See 1 Corinthians 1:18-25.) Should this affect the way our children are 'taught'?

The Spirit of the Law

Thought for the day

Jesus has the words of eternal life – he sheds light on a right attitude to the Law.

Things to read

Deuteronomy 5:6-21
2 Corinthians 3:5-11
Mark 2:23-3:6

Things to do

Using a softball play French cricket. The batsperson stands in the centre with the others in a circle, passing the ball and throwing it to aim at the batsperson's legs. If they hit them, they take a turn in the centre.

First read the passage from Deuteronomy 5, and have a brief look at the ten commandments. The spirit of the whole Law is love for God and love for neighbour, and in an effort to protect them and uphold them well, the teachers of the Law had got hung up on all the details and had lost sight of the real spirit of the Law.

Now go on to read today's Gospel, looking out for the way Jesus is going to deal with this over-zealous keeping of the letter of the Law, while shutting out the loving spirit of it. At what level are the teachers correct about Jesus breaking the Law, and at what level are they mistaken? Notice how Jesus doesn't draw away from doing what is right, even when it makes him dangerously unpopular with the authorities; never does he compromise God's values in order to protect his position.

Finally look at 2 Corinthians 3:5-11, in which Paul compares the Law written on stone with the Spirit at work in Christian hearts and lives.

Things to discuss

1. 'Love God and do what you like.' Is this a helpful way of looking at the commandments, or should we be taking the actual laws more seriously than we do?
2. What do you think might horrify Jesus today in the world, in the Church and in our own lives?

Truth and Traditions

Thought for the day

We need to be careful never to replace the timeless commands of God with man-made traditions.

Things to read

Deuteronomy 6:1-9
James 1:17-27
Mark 7:1-8, 14-15, 21-23

Things to do

On separate pieces of card write down various traditions, which they sort into 'Very important', 'Non-essential' and 'Chuck'. Here are some ideas: Christmas pudding; a white wedding; wearing black at funerals; school uniform; dinner before dessert; milk poured in before the tea; standing for the national anthem; salt and vinegar with chips; homework; wearing best clothes to church; ladies first.

Lots of our traditions are so much part of life that we only notice them when we travel abroad and find they're not there. Sometimes we take it for granted that anything we're used to doing must be right. Today we're going to look at that and question it, as Jesus did.

First read the passage from Deuteronomy, reminding them of the basic principles of the Law – Love God and love one another. Make a list of the advantages of having traditions in place to help keep the Law.

Now read the Gospel passage from Mark 7, picking out the dangers and disadvantages of having intricately worked-out traditional customs. What had happened to the way the people thought of religious duty?

Finally read from James, where we are taken back to basics, in line with what Jesus taught. How is true religion described? Talk over the traditions of our own church, looking at what is obviously very precious and important, and what seems to them to be rather in line with some of the religious teachers' rules and regulations.

Things to discuss

1. What might Jesus take offence at in the Church today which claims to be the Body of Christ?
2. Do we still accept Jesus' teaching that the 'uncleanness' which so often leads to sin comes from the inside of people, or is responsibility for sin being replaced by genetics and other circumstances beyond our control?

Discrimination

Thought for the day

Jesus overcame prejudice and discrimination and can help us to do the same.

Things to read

Proverbs 22:1-2, 8-9, 22-23
James 2:1-10
Mark 7:24-30

Things to do

Size, shape, colour. All work together (or in smaller groups) on the puzzle shown below. No adjoining shapes can have more than one thing in common.

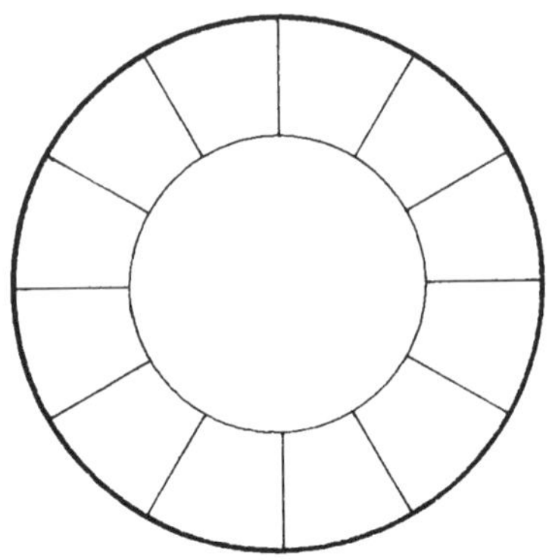

Possible solution

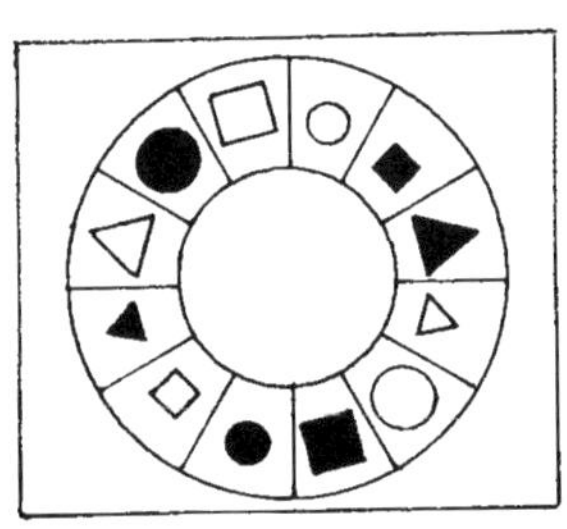

Being able to discriminate between things is an important skill which we need to have. But often our society is full of discrimination of the wrong sort, selecting those who are acceptable and those who are not; those we respect and those we can despise. There's also lots of prejudice (the word means judging before you've even met) and today's readings help us discover what Jesus' views are.

First read the passage from James, looking out for some advice for us about discrimination and prejudice. As one of the proverbs says, the thing that rich and poor have in common is that God made them both! This passage challenges our attitudes as individuals, as the Church and as members of a nation.

Now read the Gospel for today. It is about someone who was shut off, or excluded, before being welcomed in.

Things to discuss

1. How do we stand, as Church and as a nation, in relation to issues of discrimination and prejudice?

Untouchables?

Thought for the day

Jesus wants to heal us to wholeness, and to him no one is untouchable.

Things to read

Psalm 41
Mark 1:40-45

Things to do

On separate pieces of card, write out the following: a tramp; a mother with a noisy baby; a white man; a black man; a person with flu; a person with leprosy; a tattooed skinhead; a pretty girl; a handsome young man; an old lady who smells; a smoker; a disabled person; someone from a rival school.

Spread these cards out and let the group suggest a rating of 1-10 for their response to this question in each case: 'Would you be happy sitting on a crowded bus next to . . . ?'

In the activity we could see that most of us have hang-ups about close contact with people in certain situations, for all kinds of reasons. It's easy to see why society clubs together to isolate certain groups, treating them as outsiders. Our readings today help us to see what God's attitude is to social outcasts and 'untouchables'.

Begin by reading the Gospel from Mark 1. Point out that in law this man was ritually unclean, and anyone touching him would be considered contaminated, and therefore unclean themselves. What was Jesus showing by touching the leper as part of the healing? Was it just the leprosy he was healing, or would the man have also been emotionally healed in some way by the touch?

Jesus' great desire to help the man to wholeness obviously overcame any thoughts of contamination; he reckoned it worth being 'contaminated', worth being thought 'unclean'. How does that link up with the idea of the Incarnation – 'Word of the Father, now in flesh appearing'? What does it all tell us about God and his attitude to us?

Now look at Psalm 41 to get the view of a man who is shunned by others.

People who work with the rejected consider it a privilege as well as a responsibility. You could invite someone who is working in such an area to join the group. This week's teaching could well lead the group on to think of ways they can get more actively involved with local projects.

Things to discuss

1. Are there habits of social behaviour we have become so used to that we fail to see in them the marginalisation and degradation which is going on?
2. Do we ignore injustice when to act or speak out might make us unpopular? As Christians, what can we do about this?

Resisting Temptation

Thought for the day

In order to resist temptation you need to be well prepared.

Things to read

1 Corinthians 10:12-13
Hebrews 4:14-16
Mark 9:42-48

Things to do

Press flour into a pudding basin with a coin somewhere inside and carefully upend it so you have a pudding-shape of flour. People take turns at slicing the 'pudding' without making it collapse, and without dislodging the coin. Continue until one of those things happens, and the one who was cutting a slice at the time has to clear it all away. But they can keep the coin!

Today we're looking at resisting temptation. If we're not well prepared for it, we're more likely to find our good intentions collapsing in a cloud of dust, like our flour pudding. We're taking temptation seriously because Jesus did. He was tempted very severely just after his Baptism, during his ministry and in the garden of Gethsemane, just before he was arrested, and he urgently warned his disciples to watch and pray so that they wouldn't give way to temptation. They didn't realise how important it was, and ended up scattering, and leaving Jesus when he most needed them.

Begin by reading today's Gospel, from Mark 9, picking up on how seriously Jesus is wanting us to take this teaching. He uses strong, violent examples to make us think, and to help us recognise what a real battle it can be to resist evil; it isn't something to treat casually because the effects are so lasting and so damaging, both to ourselves and others, not just in this life but after death as well. Jesus is suggesting that we take strong action to turn our backs on temptation before it drags us into sin. As soon as a sin looks attractive to us – tempting – our danger lights should start flashing and that's when we need to take action. If we don't, the temptation will just get stronger, and harder to resist.

Temptation is well worth resisting, because sin is long-term destructive. Our job as Christians is to be preservers of eternal life, like salt preserves food.

Now look at the passages from 1 Corinthians and Hebrews. They tell us what help and encouragement we can receive when facing temptation.

Things to discuss

1. Do we believe that Jesus really was tempted as we are?
2. Jesus is very serious about not leading the vulnerable into sin. What can we actively do in our society as those concerned for the eternal wellbeing of souls?

Responsible and Faithful

Thought for the day

God asks of us responsibility and faithfulness in caring for our world and in our relationships.

Things to read

Genesis 2:15-24
Mark 10:2-12

Things to do

Play consequences. Each section is written and passed on around the circle, before the disjointed stories are read out. (Girl) met (boy) at (place). He said to her (. . .), she said to him (. . .), and the consequence was (. . .).

Practically every book, film and soap is about people and their relationships, falling in and out of love, marrying, divorcing, quarrelling, making up and messing up. Today we are going to look at what the Bible teaches us about faithfulness and responsibility, both with one another and with the natural world.

Begin by reading the passage from Genesis, looking at the way humankind, in the person of Adam, is placed in a position of responsibility, to care for the world and look after it. Notice how lifelong partnership is seen as God's way of providing us with companionship and help, as we work under God's rule for the good of the world.

Now read today's Gospel, where Jesus is teaching his disciples about divorce. He reminds them of the Genesis passage we have just read, reinforcing that God's way of faithfulness and responsibility in a lifelong relationship is good and rewarding. What does that mean for us as Christians, living in a time of easy divorce? It means we're going to need really serious thought and lots of prayer as we go about choosing a partner with whom we're expecting to have to spend the rest of our life, through the difficult times and broken nights, and financial worries and growing children, as well as the high spots and romantic bliss!

Things to discuss

1. How can we exercise our responsibility in caring for creation?
2. How can we ensure that we take Jesus' teaching on marriage seriously, while recognising that some marriages cause such pain and damage?

Index of Uses

TOPICS

BIBLE REFERENCES